BLACK MIRROR

BLACK MIRROR

The Selected Poems of
Roger Gilbert-Lecomte

Foreword by
Antonin Artaud
Translated by
David Rattray

Station Hill

Published by Station Hill Press, Inc., Barrytown, New York 12507 with grateful acknowledgement to the National Endowment for the Arts, a federal agency in Washington, D.C., and to the New York State Council on the Arts, for partial financial support of this project.

Produced by the Institute for Publishing Arts, Barrytown, New York 12507, a not-for-profit, tax-exempt organization.

Distributed by the Talman Company, 150 Fifth Avenue, New York, New York 10011.

A brief selection of these translations has appeared in *Symposium* magazine and *The Literary Review*.

The translator would like to acknowledge the kind assistance of the following persons: Mme. Pierre Minet, Georges Minet, Michel Carassou, Gerrit Lansing, Leonard Schwartz and Jeffra Ruesink.

Designed by Susan Quasha.

Library of Congress Cataloging-in-Publication Data

Gilbert-Lecomte, Roger, 1907-1943.
   [Poems. English. Selections]
   Black Mirror : the selected poems of Roger Gilbert-Lecomte / foreword by Antonin Artaud ; translated by David Rattray.
     p. cm.
   Includes bibliographical references.
   ISBN 0-88268-129-X. — ISBN 0-88268-128-1
   1. Gilbert-Lecomte, Roger, 1907-1943—Translations, English.
I. Title.
PQ2613.I34A2   1991   90-48769
841'.912—dc20   CIP

Manufactured in the United States of America.

BLACK MIRROR

Contents (French)

Contents (English)

Foreword—1934*

Contrary to all that has been said and done over the past fifteen or twenty years, it now appears that we must return to a definition of poetry as a thing that *sounds,* albeit mysteriously and in accordance with the laws of the quarter tone.

In Roger Gilbert-Lecomte's poems that hallow the presence of the void and the mystery of the flowing wind, there is the presence of a hidden harmony that is revealed only by its sharp edges, even in the amusing parts, even in the poems made up of a few scattered words and sounds in search of a meaning.

So barely and at times almost imperceptibly is this harmony indicated that it occasionally seems that one might doubt its very existence. This book is a window on a poetic universe, a sort of psychic star map, a magnetic compass-card aligning itself and us with all manner of waves and currents. It is the work of a man who is looking for a path, *the* path, and finds it.

Roger Gilbert-Lecomte marks the tempo, tone, nuance. He is in pitch. He discovers the real poetry, which arises from Creation and Chaos, —when poetry does not to some degree embody Anarchy, when it lacks the scale of fire and incandescence and magnetic turbulence that mark a nascent cosmos, it isn't poetry at all, for poetry's point of departure is precisely Genesis and Chaos.

The finest of these poems, the ones where the true personality of Roger Gilbert-Lecomte shines forth and unfolds, are those which deal with emptiness and wind, and secondarily with death.

In these poems a form of true lyricism — modern lyricism — makes its appearance. And in them Roger Gilbert-Lecomte breaks with the poets of the present day, to recover that organic note, that organically torn mood, that fetal, dank, fiery atmosphere that has been the hallmark of true poetry in every age, deriving its force from the life force and its source from the life source.

Here, again, as in all else, the East is our teacher. The poetry of the West lacks that air of death, that stormy feeling, that air of ill-soothed spasms that characterizes, for instance, Tibetan poetry insofar as we know it. Oriental poetry grapples with the cycle of human life, which it traces from the prena-

*As a foreword I have translated Antonin Artaud's review of Roger Gilbert-Lecomte's La Vie l'Amour la Mort le Vide et le Vent (Life Love Death Void and Wind) from La Nouvelle Revue Française, No. 255 (December 1934 [Trans.]).

tal state and makes bold to follow beyond death. One of the most gripping of these poems is the one in which Roger Gilbert-Lecomte describes the spiritual downfall of a soul that has allowed itself to be lured into the snare of reincarnation.*

The theme is a common one in the high poetry of Tibet, yet the lyricism and the accent are Roger Gilbert-Lecomte's.

Roger Gilbert-Lecomte is one of the rare poets of this century to cultivate such a form of violent, tortuous, oppressive lyricism, a lyricism made up of the screams of a man being flayed alive, clad in abrupt, elliptical language, power images whose spasms and convulsions render the groans of Nature in the throes of childbirth. Dance-of-death imagery, grave sonorities, muffled timbres spiralling in on themselves, all these mark two or three of the poems. And in an age that is more antipoetic than any that has proceeded it, one in which the writing of poetry seems a lost secret, a genuine poet has been revealed at last.

Taking a leaf from the most exalted poet-seers of Far Eastern tradition, Roger Gilbert-Lecomte's poems are at a level where metaphysics and poetry are identical. They go back to the primorial wellsprings of all imagery. They are infused with the knowledge that poetry springs from the same violent source as love and death. Roger Gilbert-Lecomte draws near that source and draws us with him.

The Orient never committed the error of indulging in personal poetry. All Oriental poetry of any value deals with universality. And personal poets (if there are any) are automatically excluded from the tradition. In Roger Gilbert-Lecomte's poetry there is a hint of something like nostalgia for a lost tradition, and the distant echo of certain grand mystical outbursts, of the menacing thunder that rumbles up out of the pages of Jacob Boehme or Novalis. That is the highest compliment I can pay, and it dispenses me from the necessity of saying anything further.

Antonin Artaud

* "Coronation and Massacre of Love," pp. 14-23 (Trans.)

Introduction

On December 31, 1943 Roger Gilbert-Lecomte died at age 36 in a Paris hospital from tetanus caused by a dirty needle. His possessions were all in one small briefcase in the room where he had been living, the back room of a working-class bar whose owner Mme. Firmat had taken him in three years before out of kindness. To Lecomte's friend the playwright Arthur Adamov she gave the briefcase. It was filled with letters, prose writings, and a hundred poems. A morphine addict, Lecomte had been jabbing the needle into a thigh muscle through a pair of dirty trousers.

Born in Reims in 1907, Lecomte was the co-founder, with René Daumal and Roger Vailland, of the literary and artistic movement Le Grand Jeu. Three issues of the group's magazine, *Le Grand Jeu,* appeared between 1928 and 1930. The Surrealists reacted to Le Grand Jeu with hostility. The group fell apart in 1932.

Central to Le Grand Jeu was a vision of the unity of everything in the universe that resulted from experiments with carbon tetrachloride performed by Lecomte with his friend René Daumal when they were teenagers. Daumal later wrote about the experience in his essay, "A Fundamental Experiment." Lecomte defined its essence as "the impersonal instant of eternity in emptiness." This glimpse of eternity in the void was to send Daumal to Hinduism, the study of Yoga philosophy, and Sanskrit. It sent Lecomte on an exploration of what he called a "metaphysics of absence." In imagination he returned to a pre-natal state, "a wondrous prior existence."

In 1933 Lecomte published a volume titled *La Vie l'Amour la Mort le Vide et le Vent* (*Life Love Death Void and Wind*), which went unnoticed by the press, save for a rave review by Antonin Artaud in the *Nouvelle Revue Française*. (Artaud's review of Lecomte is reprinted here, as a foreword to the present book.)

Over the rest of his life, Lecomte published here and there in literary magazines. His only other book was a tiny volume, *Le Miroir Noir* (*Black Mirror*), privately printed in a limited edition in 1938. The last half-dozen poems appearing in the present volume appeared in *Le Miroir Noir*. Lecomte never explained what he meant by the title. He may have been thinking of the obsidian mirrors of the Aztecs, or perhaps of the black mirrors some painters are said to use to study tonal relationships of colors seen in nature, a kind of mirror that his contemporary Francis Ponge was soon to compare to a summer sky in which he imagined he could glimpse the blackness of interstellar space. No doubt Lecomte was also thinking of his own exploration in *Le Miroir Noir* of the mind's dark side, "the dark on the blind side of mirrors."*

In later years Lecomte lived on and off with a German Jewish refugee named Ruth Kronenberg whom he had met on her arrival in Paris in 1934. She was arrested in 1940 after the Fall of France, but got out of jail, obtained false I.D., and emigrated to the Unoccupied Zone in the hope of finding safety there. In 1942 she was arrested by the collaborationist military near Carcassone, transported to the concentration camp of Drancy in the German-occupied North, and from there to Auschwitz, where she died. One of Lecomte's last publications in his lifetime was in the nature of a poignant afterthought: a twelve-line poem, "Vacancy in glass," which he retitled "Palace of the void" for publication in the *Nouvelle Revue Française,* where it appeared shortly after Ruth was deported. It seems possible that the retitled poem in its new context may reflect this personal loss.

Lecomte himself never left Paris after the early 1930's. His life was a succession of jail and hospital confinements. Very few old friends would have anything to do with him during the last years. Over the generation following his death, Lecomte's *oeuvre* acquired the status of an underground classic. His friend Adamov published a selection of his poetry, and leading French literary magazines devoted space to him. The complete works were issued in three volumes during the 1970's by Gallimard. They consist of approximately 100 poems, a booklength collection of prose texts, including essays setting forth the principles of the Grand Jeu movement and various pieces of literary criticism, and, finally, a volume of letters.

Lecomte had an intimation that at the prime origin of things there stirred something like a breath of wind. This he hoped would fill him. The Isha Upanishad contains a prayer to be recited at the moment of death: *Breath enter immortal wind*. That prayer is implicit in all that he ever wrote.

David Rattray

*"Holy Childhood or Concealment of Birth," pp. 90–93.

On Translating Lecomte

To translate is to transpose. Sometimes one settles for an equivalent. This should leap forth like the rabbit from the magician's sleeve.

Lecomte imbibed the grand manner with his ABC's. His own style however rips the grand manner to shreds. High, low, and middle levels of usage are deliberately scrambled, as though he wished to plunge through the surface into the dimension of emptiness and silence underlying it.

For instance: Lecomte cultivated the sonnet. The four sonnets appearing in this book could have been rendered in a reshaped form, handling the original as Stravinsky handled Gesualdo. I elected not to. The sonnet was quite as archaic in the France of 1930 as it is in the U.S.A. of today. Sonnet *form,* however, opens out and closes in a fashion peculiar to itself and uniquely suited to those four poems.

In all of Lecomte's poetry, the line is the basic unit. Each line in English must work the same as its equivalent in the French original. Oftener than not, the syntax comes out altogether different.

Take for example "La Sagesse Inutile," whose title I render "A Sagacious but Unprofitable Observation." This poem about lice is one of those "amusing parts" that Artaud's preface mentions. To get across, it must come trippingly off the tongue like a limerick. The mock-pompous title sets it up in a way the literally translated "Useless Wisdom" would not.

"Shampoo" follows. My first rule is to understand the text I am translating. Line one reads: *Incense clings to the Corpse's abdomen.* I understand the line in the light of Jesus' saying that this world is a corpse. In other words, corporeal existence here below has a lingering fragrance. It doesn't just simply stink. I had to search high and low for the proper rendering of *Allah est grand.* A bumper sticker gave "Great is Allah!" The sentence *Mais moi je suis héautophobe très hyperesthésiquement,* with its echo of Baudelaire's *héautotimoroumenos* and the fact that modern French, unlike present-day American English, generates learned compounds with tireless zest, had me on the ropes until I remembered Rene Ricard's lines: *I was born to live for him, to die for him. Now I could kill him.* My rendering of the poem's conclusion became *Not I, for I was born to loathe myself and drink through my thin skin evening's hope and the naked fright of dawn.*

Another short poem, "Il est infiniment regrettable," would fall flat on its face as "It is infinitely regrettable." A juicy equivalent is "What a howling shame ... " In the opening of the same poem, to translate *désuétude* as "desuetude" or "obsolescence" would obscure rather than illuminate. The phrase *machine à feu* means combustion machine but *pyrological machine* is far better. The "Trinity" it is based upon I embody in a triad of alliterations:

spunk - spirit - spectre.

The original has *instrument de valeur magique* and *magie poétique* which I render as "a magical instrument of incalculable poetic and shamanic value." Spacing renders phrasing.

The standard text for Gilbert-Lecomte's poems is the edition established by Jean Bollery, forming volume two of the Complete Works in the Gallimard edition of 1977. For a number of poems, there are variants. Some of these occur in the original edition of Gilbert-Lecomte, *Testament* (1955), edited by Arthur Adamov, also published, but subsequently withdrawn, by Gallimard. Others may be found in an edition of several Lecomte poems edited by Claudio Rugafiori, published by Fata Morgana in 1977 under the title (it had been a projected title of Gilbert-Lecomte's) *Caves en plein ciel* (Cellars in the Sky). From the discussions of the manuscripts and of their respective methods of dealing with them, Bollery and Rugafiori make it clear that much of the material has had to be reconstructed from a manuscript full of changes, erasures, lacunae, inserts of uncertain destination, and variants of differing weight or intent. I was helped in this by the detailed discussions of variants appearing in *Roger Gilbert-Lecomte et le Grand Jeu* (1981), by Alain and Odette Virmaux. Since my primary consideration in making this English-language version was to create poems that could be effectively re-cited or read out loud to an audience, I studied the various possible alternative versions and made judgments and choices on poetic grounds. The poem that opens the present selection is a case in point. In it, I have inserted stanzas that occur in the texts of Adamov and Rugafiori, but only in the back matter of Bollery. I put them in because in my opinion they make a better poem in English.

In recreating a foreign-language poem in English, my general rule is that the translation must sound the way the original poet would sound if he or she were me. The most trying moments spent with this particular poet have been those when a phrase such as "the dream's golden branch" clunks down in the middle of a text of otherwise arresting immediacy, like a cluster of baroque ornamentation in the middle of a ballade by let's say Sonny Clark. Then it dawns on me that Roger Gilbert-Lecomte is pulling my leg.

D.R.

BLACK MIRROR

Tablettes d'un visionné

Je suis mort. De plus en plus.
« Petit mort pour rire! » — Oui, suis
devenu si petit que tiendrais tout entier
dans le fourneau de ma ridiculement
minuscule petite pipe en bois.

Ils m'appellent Ismaël, père
Ismaël, mais suis si petit que ce
doit être pour se moquer.

Étant mort,
                              je vis très légèrement.

Il fait noir,
                              et froid.

Froid : L'aube d'une nouvelle
période glaciaire. Un mystique
transi sous des palmes gelées. Blancheur
de faiblesses.

Noir : Un rat roide, — vertical, —
en équilibre sur l'extrême bout de
sa queue chauve. Qui hurle à la
mort sans faire bouger son museau.

Froid : Dans une plaine (vert-amande)
une longue file d'éléphants d'un
pâle bleu marche à reculons.

Noir — un long petit rat voltige
avec des ailes de libellule.

Froid : une petit tête violette
grimace, dans la transparence du
ventre bombé d'une amphore.

Noir : Deux formes humaines —
absolument identiques, — se tuent en
se baisant sur la bouche.

Froid : Un buste d'homme tronqué
se fait comprendre en clignant ses
paupières.

Noir — Au-dessus de nuages ou de
sombres sables. S'érigent les symboles

Notes for a Coming Attraction

I died. Deader and deader.
"Little joke corpse!" Yeah, I
shrank beyond belief; I'd even fit quite neatly
inside the bowl of my ridiculously
miniscule briarwood pipe.
    Ishmael they call me, Father
Ishmael. I'm such a pipsqueak, though,
they have got to be kidding.
    Being dead means
                  very light housekeeping.
    It's dark,
                 and cold.
Cold as the dawn of a new
Ice Age. A sage frostbitten
under gelid palmtrees. The pallor
of one's foibles.
    Dark: A rat standing
at attention on the tip of his
hairless tail squealing bloody
murder without the slightest movement of his snout.
    Cold: Across an almond-green plain
a procession of pale blue elephants
walking backwards.
    Dark: A diminutive stringbean of a rat hovers
on dragonfly wings.
    Cold: A wee purple face glares out of a winejar's
bulging glassy midriff.
    Dark: Two perfectly identical human mouths
kiss each other to death.
    Cold: A truncated male torso
gives with a significant wink.
    Dark: Above clouds or
black sands. Idols of old religions
set up. Facing them,
horror in tar: the grin of certain dead people.
    Cold . . .—Polar . . .— I'm entombed

divins des vieilles religions. En face,
horreur macadamisée : les rictus de
certains trépassés.

    Froid : . . . — Polaire . . . — Suis enseveli
sous les neiges. Toutes les étoiles,
cruelles! — d'une voix lointaine et
féminine chantent le cantique :

> « Au ciel, au ciel, au ciel
> J'irai La voir un jour . . . »

    Noir : Une monstrueuse petite bedaine
contemplant le monde extérieur avec
le regard de son nombril ahuri.

    Froid : Le ruban cramoisi —
laide cravate au cou d'une
plante de serre — bat soudain
comme un coeur.

    Froid :   Gérard de Nerval.
                            Nu. Dans la nuit pure.
                            Attend que son âme
                            Monte vers l'étoile.

    Noir : Trois poissons phosphorescents
remontent, par saccades, le cours
lourd d'un fleuve noir.

                  Cela passe.

                  Mais suis si petit, —
je crois que je diminue encore, —
si petit que vraiment . . .

in snows. The stars all out,—
how cruel they are!—female voices
singing in the distance:
                    In heaven, heaven, heaven
                    I'll see Her bye and bye . . .
    Dark: A monstrous little potbelly
considering the surface of reality with the
gaze of its flabbergasted belly button.
    Cold: The crimson ribbon. Ugly necktie
round the neck of a hothouse plant—
suddenly beating like a heart.
    Cold: Gérard de Nerval
                    Nude. In pure night sky.
                    Waits for his soul to
                    Fly up to its star.

    Dark: Three phosphorescent fish
leap up a dark stream's
slow course.

                    It passes.

                    Me being so tiny, though,—

I think I'm still shrinking,—
so tiny that in fact . . .

Nuit de bal

Un bureau de tabac sur une place de
                                village
Bravant le mépris de la « jeune fille
qui n'a pas d'épaules » j'y vole deux
écarlates boîtes de cigarettes.

Fuite sur une route rectiligne.
Vautré dans une voiture à bras qui
roule d'elle-même.
Jusqu'à un croisement de route.

Cent mètres à pieds.
Maison solitaire dans la campagne
  « TAVERNE ALGÉROISE »
J'entre avec la nuit finissante.

Rez de chaussée.
Sombre : on boit sur des barriques
Escalier de meunier.
Vers le premier étage. Salle enfumée et populeuse
Où, conflagration de la Rencontre.
Vers moi le Magicien
(Jeune oriental vêtu à l'européenne)
je participe à son être
Oh, ses passes et ses yeux d'envoûtement
à jamais sur mon âme.

                    L'oubli décolore le reste . . .

Incantatoires apothéoses indicibles car:
L'angoisse des caves de ténèbres.
soeur de mes veilles et sommeils
S'exalte, se divinise et se métempsycose
En la très rare extase d'Angoisse
(qui n'est pas d'un mortel.)

Dance Night

In a cigar store on the main square
                    of a country town

I brave the contempt of "that girl with no
shoulders" and stealing 2
scarlet boxes of cigarettes

make my getaway
hunched over a handcar
                    running on its own momentum
as far as the next crossing

where I go 100 yards on foot
to a house standing by itself
         ALGERIA TAVERN
I go inside, it's the dead of night

Ground floor is dark, they are drinking at tables made of casks
I go up a narrow flight of stairs
to the second floor, a crowded smoke-filled room

where (flash encounter)
toward me the Magician
young oriental in western dress
he resembles me
oh those hypnotic eyes and passes
forever branded on the back of my mind

            The rest fades into oblivion . . .
Casting of spells—Apotheoses—things that can't be said:
The anguish I knew in the caves of darkness
sister of my every waking and sleeping moment
arises in glory and transmigrates
into a most rare
(no longer mortal) ecstasy of pain

Au fond le plus reculé de mes
          cauchemars oubliés
C'est une étanche cellule d'où diffuse
Toute la lumière originelle

(Son intensité inondant un
aveugle vivant voilé de noir
         le tuerait.)

C'est tout ce qu'il m'a permis de
dire.

at the bottom of the most utterly
            forgotten nightmares
an airtight cell, out of which
primal light flashes

(the full force of it, flooding a living
man, even if blind and draped in black,
            would kill)

That's all he let me say

Il est infiniment regrettable

Il est infiniment regrettable
Que la désuétude
efface l'usage
Du briquet d'amadou
Machine à feu
basée sur la Trinité

Du fantôme de l'amadou
De l'esprit du silex
Du spectre de l'acier
Instrument de valeur magique
De magie poétique
      incalculable
      inappréciable

What a Howling Shame

What a howling shame
progress
has eliminated the usage
of the tinderbox
that pyrological machine
based on the Trinity

From the phantom of spunk
the spirit of flint
and the spectre of steel
a magical instrument
of incalculable
poetic and shamanic value

Les frontières de l'amour

Entre les lèvres du baiser
La vitre de la solitude

The Borders of Love

Between two mouths in a kiss
Windowglass.

Sacre et massacre de l'amour

I

A l'orient pâle où l'éther agonise
A l'occident des nuits des grandes eaux
Au septentrion des tourbillons et des tempêtes
Au sud béni de la cendre des morts

Aux quatre faces bestiales de l'horizon
Devant la face du taureau
Devant la face du lion
Devant la face de l'aigle
Devant la face d'homme inachevée toujours
Et sans trêve pétrie par la douleur de vivre

Au coeur de la colombe
Dans l'anneau du serpent

Du miel du ciel au sel des mers

Seul symbole vivant de l'espace femelle
Corps de femme étoilé
Urne et forme des mondes

Corps d'azur en forme de ciel

II

Territoire fantôme des enfants de la nuit
Lieu de l'absence du silence et des ombres
Tout l'espace et ce qu'il enserre
Est un trou noir dans le blanc plein

Comme la caverne des mondes
Tout le corps de la femme est un vide à combler

Coronation and Massacre of Love

I

To the pale east in the agony of ether
To the west in the night of great waters
To the septentrion in back of the north wind
To the south blest by the ashes of the dead

To the four animal faces of the cardinal points
To the face of the bull
To the lion's face
To the eagle's face
To the forever unfinished and ever agonized
Human face

At the heart of a dove
In a snake's coil

From the honey of heaven to the salt of the ocean sea

Of the icons meaning female space only one lives
It is a woman's body made up of stars
A shape and vessel holding the universe

A blue skinned body formed like the sky

II

A home to ghosts and to the children of night
A place of absence stillness gloom
The whole of space and what it holds
In a field all white a black hole

Like the cave of the sky
The whole body of woman is a vacuum to be filled

III

L'aube froide
Des ténèbres pâles
Inonde les pôles
Du ciel et de la chair

Des courants souterrains de la chair et des astres

Au fond des corps de terre
Les tremblements de terre
Et les failles où vont les volcans du délire
Tonner

Entez sur le trépieds
Celle qui hurle
La bouche mangée
Par l'amertume
En flammes du laurier de gloire
Écume
De la colère des mers
La femme à chevelure
D'orages
Aux yeux d'éclipse
Aux mains d'étoiles rayonnantes
A la chair tragique vêtue de la soie des frissons
A la face sculptée au marbre de l'effroi
Aux pieds de lune et de soleil
A la démarche d'océan
Aux reins mouvants de vive houle
Ample et palpitante

Son corps est le corps de la nuit
Flamme noire et double mystère
De son inverse identité qui resplendit
Sur le miroir des grandes eaux

III

In a cloak of pale shadow
Cold dawn
Floods sky and living flesh
From pole to pole

From the occult currents common to flesh and stars

To the bottom of each earthy body
Earthquake
And fault through which a volcano of madness
Roars

Nail that screaming woman
To the tripod
Her mouth consumed
In the flaming
Glory of the bitter laurel
Foams
Like a raging sea
Her hair is a
Hurricane
Her eyes an eclipse
Stars are streaming out of her fingertips
Her tragic flesh draped in a silk of tremors
Her face carved in the marble of fright
Her feet the sun and moon
She strides along like an ocean
Rolling her hips
In a long ample pulsing swell

Her body embodying the night
Black flame the double mystery
Of an inverse identity
Shimmering in the mirror of great waters

IV

Visitation blême au désert de l'amour

Aveugle prophétesse au regard de cristal
Que les oreilles de ton coeur
Entendent rugir les lions intérieurs
Du coeur

Le grand voile de brume rouge et la rumeur
Du sang brûlé par le poison des charmes

Et les prestiges du désir
Suscitant aux détours de ta gorge nocturne
La voracité des vampires

Danse immense des gravitations nuptiales
Aux palpitations des mondes et des mers
Au rythme des soleils du coeur et des sanglots
Vers le temple perdu dans l'abîme oublié
Vers la caverne médusante qu'enfanta
L'ombre panique dans la première nuit du monde
Voici l'appel la trombe et le vol des semences
L'appel au fond de tout du centre souterrain

Danseuse unissant la nuit à l'eau-mère
Végétal unissant la terre au sang du ciel

V

Comme Antée reprend vie au contact de la terre
Le vide reprend vie au contact de la chair

Je viens dans ton sein accomplir le rite

IV

In the desert of love a glimmering visitation

Blind prophetess your eye has the clarity of cut glass
Let the ear of your heart
Hear the lion growl
Within

Veiled in a red fog and the buzz
Of blood seared by the venomous spells
And prestigia of desire
Exciting in the bend of your nocturnal throat
The voracity of vampires

Vast dance of nuptial gravitations whole
Worlds and seas pulsing
To the heartbeat of a weeping sun
Down into the temple lost in the forgotten deep
Down into the medusa hole that first spawned
A panic shadow on the first night of the creation
Hear the trumpet blast and the scattered seed
Blasting all the way to bedrock at the bottom of the deepest cave

She dances to connect night and mother sea
A plant connecting earth and the blood of heaven

V

As Antaeus revives by touching earth
To revive empty space by touching skins

In your bosom I lie in order to perform the rite
Of homecoming to where I came from when not yet born
The animal sign of the archaic ecstasy

Le rythmique retour au pays d'avant-naître
Le signe animal de l'extase ancienne

Je viens dans ton sein déposer l'offrande
Du baume et du venin

Aveugle anéanti dans les caves de l'être

VI

Mais qui saurait forcer le masque de ta face
Et l'opaque frontière des peaux
Atteindre le point nul en soi-même vibrant
Au centre le point mort et père des frissons
Roulant à l'infini leurs ondes circulaires
Tout immobile au fond du coeur l'astre absolu
Le point vide support de la vie et des formes
Qui deviennent selon le cercle des tourments
Le secret des métamorphoses aveugles

D'où vient l'espoir désespéré
D'amour anéanti dans une double absence
Au sommet foudroyé du délire
Acte androgyne d'unité
Que l'homme avait à jamais oublié
Avant la naissance du monde

Avant l'hémorragie
Avant la tête

VII

Paroles du Thibet
Il est dit autrefois
Qu'errant éperdue dans l'informe
Éparse dans l'obscurité
La pauvre ombre sans graisse du mort

In your bosom I lay the offering
Of balm and venom mixed

Blind as I am
In the caves of being that are the antechambers of annihilation

VI

Yet who could peel the mask off your face
And the skin's opaque frontier
To reach the quivering fulcrum of the self
That point at dead center of the eye
Of an endlessly expanding series of rings
Itself perfectly motionless at the bottom of the heart star of the absolute
Empty point foundation of all life and of the forms
Which according to the circle of torments
Become the secret of blind change

Whence the desperation
Of a love canceled in a double absence
At the thunderstruck peak of delirium
An act of androgynous unity
The man had forgotten forever already
Before the universe had even begun to exist

Before hemorrhage
Before head

VII

In the Tibetan story
Lost in chaos unkempt and
Darkness like a
Mouthful of dirt

A dead person's fatless shade
Whirls in black oblivion shivering

La bouche pleine de terre
Dans le noir sans mémoire tourbillonne il fait froid
L'espace ne connaît que le glissement glacé des larves
Soudain
Si phalène que tente une lueur lointaine
Elle aperçoit la caverne enchantée
Le paradis illuminé des gemmes chaudes
Le règne des splendeurs et des béatitudes
Aux confins du désir essentiel
Qui jamais satisfait perpétuel se comble

A l'appel enivrant d'odeurs vertigineuses
Qu'elle y entre
Ombre morte
Et s'endorme
Pour se réveiller à jamais enchaînée
Engluée aux racines d'un ventre
Foetus hideux voué pour une vie encore
Au désespoir des générations
Roulé par la roue de l'horreur de vivre

Du vieux foetus aïeul
A notre mère putride
La pourriture aïeule
En robe de phosphore

La reine démente
Qui fait et défait
Le destins et les formes

Et du corps étoilé
De l'éternelle femme
Livre les ossements à l'honneur de la cendre

Impose à l'orgueil de statue des chairs
L'horizontalité effroyable de l'eau

For the icy slithering of ghosts is all there is out there
When suddenly it finds itself
Drawn to a distant glimmer then
Looking into an enchanted cave
A light-filled paradise of warm jewels
A little kingdom of splendors and beatitudes
In the region known as essence of desire
Which though never sated is forever satisfied

Lured by the exhilarating smell
The shade
Enters
And sleeps
Only to awake riveted
Rooted in a uterus
A ghastly fetus doomed to one more round
Of procreative desperation
Spinning on the wheel of the horror of existence

All the way back from the eldest fetal ancestor
To the putrid mother of us all
Our first ancester rot
In her robe of foxfire

The demented queen
Who makes and unmakes
Forms and fortunes

And by committing the eternal feminine
Star-studded bones and all
To the honor of ash

Imposes on skin's
Statuesque and prideful inclination
Water's dread horizontality

La sagesse inutile

L'homme cherche l'amour et le pou cherche l'homme
L'homme cherche le pou qui se cache prudent
Dans la forêt des poils où l'homme trébuchant
Les yeux bandés cherche l'amour colin-maillard

A Sagacious but Unprofitable Observation

You go for love and cooties go for you
Go for the cooties they wisely retreat
In the forest of hairs where stumbling pairs
Play blindman's buff with each other's muff
And all of creation's in heat

Schampoing ...

à René Daumal

Au ventre du Cadavre erre un fumet d'encens
Allah est grand! ... Mais moi je suis héautophobe
Très hyperesthésiquement et je pressens
L'espoir du crépuscule et l'effroi nu de l'aube.

Shampoo

to René Daumal

Incense clings to the Corpse's abdomen
Great is Allah! Not I for I was born
To loathe myself and drink through my thin skin
Evening's hope and the naked fright of dawn

L'aile d'endormir

Il remontait si loin le courant de sa vie
Qu'il se trouvait perdu au pays à l'envers
Où l'on erre avant la naissance

Il rêvait rêvait-il
Il changeait de planète
S'éveillant s'endormant sans cesse et tour à tour
Au tic tac cérébral de l'horloge dit sang

S'endormant chaque fois dans des sommeils plus creux

S'éveillant chaque fois plus loin dans la lumière
Plus près du feu
Plus bas dans l'eau mortelle des ténèbres

Sa couche le berçait somptueuse litière
Attelée d'épaules ailées
Puis l'immobilisait de l'arrêt dur des pierres
Que dressait son tombeau

Le va-et-vient sorcier de l'aile d'endormir
Faisait de ses yeux morts jaillir des étincelles
Puis au retour effaçait son regard

Et ses yeux repartaient en si lointain voyage
Que ses orbites se creusaient
Et crispaient comme des lèvres d'amertume ses paupières

Il se sentait grandir à devenir le ciel
Devenir le beau temps pleuvoir faire arc-en-ciel

Et puis les meules de l'espace l'écrasaient
Et l'aplatissaient comme une ombre . . .

(A suivre.)

28

The Wing of Sleep

He waded all the way back up life's stream
And came out the other side
Lost where others wander not yet born

He dreamt he was dreaming
Changing planets
Sleeping only to awake over and over
To the clock of blood ticking in his head

Plunging in an ever deeper sleep

Awaking in depths of light unmeasured
Yet closer to that blaze
Plunged in the mortal deep of shadow

His bed a sumptuous cradle whose plumed head
Rocked him
Then froze into the lintel
Of a tomb

His dead eyes the wing of the enchanter sleep
Brushed to glittering life
Then rubbed out

Into so total a revulsion
Their lids
Squinched up like spleen-envenomed lips

He felt himself expand becoming the sky
Making fair weather and foul while dispensing rainbows

As the mills of space crushed
And flattened him like a shadow . . .

(to be continued)

La vie masquée

Grande statue de femme en cire pâle et lourde
La statue qui pivote avec une lenteur effroyable
    toujours
Toupie tournant dans l'huile de dormir
Phare aux yeux fermés dont la face à éclipses
Ne projette que les rayons paralytiques de l'effroi

Grande prison de cire en forme de femme
Qui renferme muré dans le creux de son moule
Un cadavre vivant de femme
Mangeant l'intérieur de sa face de statue

A chaque tour de lenteur effroyable
Le cadavre vivant de femme muré
Pousse un seul immense cri silencieux
Qui fait imperceptiblement frémir la cire

Pour le spectateur envoûté
Au premier tour la face est masquée d'un nuage
Rouge et qui s'étire
Comme la pieuvre du sang au fond des mers

Au second tour la face apparaît noire et close
Comme un masque de suie pulvérulente et grasse

Au troisième tour avec une lenteur effroyable
La face découvre ses dents

Le spectateur s'endort

Se réveille muré
Dans le ventre vivant du cadavre moulé de cire
Dans un monde tournant de lenteur effroyable
Plein de scies et de rats

Masked Life

A massive pale waxwork of a woman
Forever rotating in horrible slow motion,
The statue spins like a top on the grease of dreams,
A blind lighthouse whose eclipsed face is
Haloed with a numb nimbus of horror

A massive wax prison in female shape
It encloses within its hollow shell
A female zombie eating away
Its sculptured face from within

Completing each revolution in horrible slow motion
The imprisoned female zombie
Lets out an immense silent shriek
Making the wax shudder imperceptibly

For the bewitched spectator of its
First revolution, the face is masked by a red cloud
From which it shrinks like an octopus from
Blood on the ocean floor

At its second revolution the face turns black,
An opaque mask of greasy dripping suet

At its third revolution in horrible slow motion
The face bares its teeth

The spectator sleeps

Only to come to, trapped
In the waxwork zombie's womb,
In a universe of ripsaws and rats
Gyrating in horrible slow motion

Le fils de l'os parle

Je frappe comme un sourd à la porte des morts
Je frappe de la tête qui gicle rouge
On me sort en bagarre on m'emmène
Au commissariat
Rafraîchissement du passage à tabac
Les vaches
Ce n'est pas moi pourtant
Qui ai commencé
A la porte des morts que je voulais forcer
Si je suis défoncé saignant stupide et blême
Et rouge par traînées
C'est que je n'ai jamais voulu que l'on m'emmène
Loin des portes de la mort où je frappais
De la tête et des pieds et de l'âme et du vide
Qui m'appartiennent et qui sont moi
Mourez-moi ou je meurs tuez-moi ou je tue
Et songez bien qu'en cessant d'exister je vous suicide
Je frappe de la tête en sang contre le ciel en creux
Au point de me trouver debout mais à l'envers
Devant les portes de la mort
Devant les portes de la mer
Devant le rire des morts
Devant le rire des mers
Secoué dispersé par le grand rire amer
Épars au delà de la porte des morts
Disparue
Mais je crie et mon cri me vaut tant de coups sourds
Qu'assommé crâne en feu tombé je beugle et mords
Et dans l'effondrement des sous-sols des racines
Tout au fond des entrailles de la terre et du ventre
Je me dresse à l'envers le sang solidifié
Et les nerfs tricoteurs crispés jusqu'à la transe
Piétinez piétinez ce corps qui se refuse
A vivre au contact des morts
Que vous êtes pourris vivants cerveaux d'ordures
Regardez-moi je monte au-dessous des tombeaux

32

Son of Bone Talks

I bang like a deaf man at death's door
I bang my head against it squirting red
They drag me away
To headquarters and
Make me eat it
The swine
But I wasn't the one that
Started it
At death's door
Okay I admit I was trying to bust in
I may be messed up all blood stupid pale
Dripping a red trail
It's only that I was never willing to be yanked
Away from that gate I was banging at
With all the head feet heart and vacuity proper to me
Do me or I'll die
Kill me or I'll kill
Though me ceasing to exist means
You're committing suicide
You'd better believe it
I bang my head on a blank sky
I get back up but I'm inside out
At the gates of the dead
At the gates of the sea
At the laughter of the dead
At the laughter of the oceans
Shook up by that bitter laughter
Cloud of confetti
On the other side
Now you see me
Now you don't
I yell and the more I yell the more they kick
Half dead my head on fire on the floor I bellow bite and
Pass out in this cellar
In the ass end of the universe and of the gut
Blood curdled skin on backwards

Jusqu'au sommet central de l'intérieur de tout
Et je ris du grand rire en trou noir de la mort
Au tonnerre du rire de la rage des morts

Nerve ends disconnected in a trance I try getting up
Stomp ahead
Stomp a body for declining
To live in contact with corpses
You know who you are shitheads
Look I zoom under the cemeteries
All the way to earth's central inner peak at the heart of it all
A black hole laughing loud
Over the raging laughter of the dead

Le grand et le petit guignol

Nous étions dans la houille et tu parlais de mort
Les destins passaient rouges en hurlant
Les moutons de la mer se suicidaient
En heurtant du crâne les roches des rives

Nous étions dans la mer et tu parlais d'embruns
Aux bulles de la mer imbuvable
Les poissons du ciel passaient aux lointains
Nous étions prisonniers des pieuvres et du sable

Nous étions dans le noir et tu parlais d'espoir
L'heure est passée il n'est plus d'heure
Le ciel renversé comme un bol se vide
Dans le trou du noir

Nous étions dans les pierres et tu parlais encore
Du sang qui fait mal et des larmes
Nous étions arrivés au tréfonds des bas-fonds
Nous étions dans les glaives

Nous étions dans le feu tu parlais du suicide
Universel

Horror Show Puppet Show

We were knee deep in coal you talked of death
Howling destinies rushed past in red
Lemmings flung themselves over the cliff
Bashing their brains out on the rocks below

We were in the ocean you said it's fizzy
Of the bubbly but undrinkable brine
As herringbones sailed past far overhead
And we lay trapped between the sand and sharks

We lay in darkness you talked of hope
The hour's past there is no more hour
Heaven inverted as a bowl empties
Itself into the hole of night

We lay over the rocks and you were still talking
Of blood that sears and all about tears
We'd got into the quicksand in the shallows
And hit the reef of coral called the swords

We roasted in the fires of hell but you
Kept saying let's all kill ourselves at once

Complainte du ludion

Sortir de son propre cadavre, identique à soi-même, en vire-voltant dru et sec.

Ce faisant, noircir tout entier et s'amincir vers les extrémités. Prendre une crinière rouge et d'immenses yeux laiteux à pupille de chat, en ligne verticale.

Flotter dans un espace comme sous-marin, vaguement limité de vieux et épais cristal aux reflets de ténèbres polychromes.

Dans ce bocal, illimité ou vaste, se mouvoir en ludion, monter et descendre, souple et emphatique, comme au ralenti.

En griffant des parois lisses avec des ongles effilés et terreux.

Cartesian Diver

The trick is to get out of your own dead body
in one piece. One quick hard twist and you're out.

Next, you turn black all over and taper at
the extremities. Grow a red mane and huge milky eyes
like a cat's, with vertical slits for pupils.

Now hover in air as if undersea, in a space
enclosed by thick walls of ancient crystal with
rich polychrome refractions.

Within this limitless or at least vast container,
move in the manner of a Cartesian diver. Rise and
sink with the supple emphasis of slow motion.

Scratch your tank's smooth sides with sharp
dirty nails.

Le pendu

Au creux de l'estomac
Toute l'angoisse du monde
Qui serre
Le noeud coulant

The Hanged Man

At the pit of the stomach
All the agony of the universe
At the service of a
Slipknot.

Le vide de verre

Un palais aux murs
De vent

Un palais dont les tours
Sont de flamme au grand jour

Un palais d'opale
Au coeur du zénith

L'oiseau fait d'air pâle
Y vole vite

Laisse une traînée blanche
Dans l'espace noir

Son vol dessine un signe
Qui signifie absence

Vacancy in Glass

To a palace made
Of wind

To a palace whose towers
Are pillars of fire by day

To an opal palace
In the sky's zenith heart

The bird of pale air
Flies

In a swift white line
On black space

A brushstroke
Signifying absence

Je n'ai pas peur du vent

Toi qui hurles sans gueule
Mords sans dents
Fascines sans yeux
Face creuse
Toi qui fais bondir la pantomime des ombres et des lumières
Coupes sans faux
Arraches claques et bats
Sans bras sans mains sans fouets sans fléau
Fléau toi-même vent levant du Levant
Toi qui mets le tonnerre au coeur de la forê
Et fais courir les géants de sable au désert
Père des vagues des cyclones des tornades
Déformant d'hystérie la face de la mer
Jusqu'à la trombe
Coït de l'eau salée et du ciel sucré
Char ailé de la dame blanche reine des tempêtes de neige
Toi qui bossues les dunes
Et les dos des chameaux
Toi qui ébouriffes la crinière des lions
Qui fais gémir les loups
Et chanter les roseaux les bambous
Les sistres et les harpes
Toi qui fais tomber les pots de fleur sur les sommets des citoyens pour leur
ouvrir la tête siège de la compréhension
Et descendre les avalanches dans les vallées pour les emplir
Toi qui berces les ailes étalées du sommeil de l'oiseau sans pattes
Qui naît en l'air
Et va se suicider aux cimes coupantes du ciel
Toi qui trousses les cottes
Et dévastes les côtes
Les côtes en falaises et les côtes en os
Toi qui horripiles les peaux
Secoues les oripeaux les drapeaux les persiennes
Les plis des manteaux des voyageurs égarés les arbres
Les fantômes et les allumettes perdus dans l'immensité
Toi qui ondules les ondes et les chevelures
Fais cligner les yeux et les flammes

I'm Not Scared of Wind

You scream without a mouth
You bite and are toothless
You stare hypnotically and have no eyes
You puff without cheeks without a face
You make shadow-plays climb walls
You slice without a cutting edge without hands or arms
You rip smack crack although
You lack a whip you are one so
You rise in the orient a levantine scourge
roaring at the dark wood's heart
You tire sand devils out over the desert
You sire seawaves cyclones hurricanes
You twist the face of the deep into a snout of hysteria
Squinching up into that spout
Saltwater and taffy sky make when they fuck in the backseat of
White lady blizzard queen's batmobile
You hump a dune soon as a
Camel's back
You ruffle a lion's mane
Make wolves groan harps moan
Toot bamboo shoots
Tinkle chimes
Tumble flowerpots onto the crowns of citizens to crack open their pate that
seat of understanding
You push avalanches down hills which fills vales
You preen the outspread pinions of sleep
a bird hatched legless in midair
about to cut its own throat on the razor's edge of heaven
You skirt lifter
You rifter of ribs
both continental and insularly human
You gooser of flesh
You flag and venetian blind and tinsel ruffler
You riffler of wrinkles on the cloaks of displaced travelers and trees
And will-o'-the-wisps and lucifers twinkling in immensity
You maker of waves wavy hair and

Claquer les oriflammes
Grand voyou chérubin démesuré
Clown des tourbillons
Sculpteur de nuages
Roi des métamorphoses
Toi qui fais vivre éperdument les choses qui sans toi
Seraient vouées à l'inertie la plus plate
Immense père des spectres et des frissons
Toi qui animes la gesticulation des rideaux mystère
Dans les châteaux hantés
En gueulant partout
Dans les couloirs les cheminées et les fosses d'aisance
Toi qui fais voyager la pluie et le beau temps
Quand ils s'ennuient
Et t'amuses à faire peur aux petits oiseaux
En agitant les épouvantails à moineaux
Polichinelles sans fils
A moins que tu n'introduises dans ces simulacres en haillons
Les âmes trémoussantes des morts de mort
Violente et criminelle
Toi qui fais tourner le lait des nourrices les aiguilles des montres les
tornades et les moulins à vent
Toi qui effrayes les enfants emmerdes les parents
Fais la joie des pirates et des voiles
Des pirouettes des feuilles
Et des girouettes que tu prends pour des girouettes
Toi par qui tremblent les trembles
Et trébuchent les vieillards pitoyables
Sans coeur Affreux Dégingandé Vicieux
Alizé mistral tramontane simoun de malheur vilain sirocco
Toi qui retournes comme des omelettes les jolis bateaux
Et les avions comme des pétales de rose
Toi qui joues aux ballons avec ceux d'entre eux
Qui ne sont pas captifs ou qui ne le sont plus
Toi qui tortilles la raideur des tuyaux de poêle
Assassin des cheminées voleur de chapeaux
Apache Jeteur de poivre aux yeux
Père du hâle qui aime les peaux Face de rat
Toi qui étires les formes
Déformes les visions

Eyes and flames that wink as
Oriflammes snap crackle and pop in the breeze
You rascal you excessive cherub
You dervish clown
You cloud sculptor
You king of change
You bring things that without you would be doomed to the most flat-footed
inertia madly alive
You engender major phantoms and fits of the willies
You are the one behind the rustling of the mystery drapes
In the haunted castle
Ubiquitous
You hoot through hallways chimneys latrines
You send fair weather and foul packing
when they get bored
You get off on frightening little birds
Watch that scarecrow jump
When you aren't inspiring
the tremulous moth-eaten wraith of a victim of
Foul play
You make mother's milk minute-hands
whirlwinds and windmills turn
You spook young exasperate old
You puff pirates' sails
Whirligigs leaves and
Weathervanes you take at face value
Letting aspens quake and
little old men dodder
Dreadful Heartless Cold Fish Creep
Monsoon mistral tramontane simoom of doom loco sirocco
You fold a ship over like an omelette
A plane like a rose petal
Playing ball with balloons
both free-floating and no longer captive
You yank the rigidity of stovepipes out of whack
You chimney toppler hat snatcher
Hooligan thrower of pepper in open eyes
Source of the weathered look you
adore skin
You distort form

Déformes les visions
Et fais aux parois de l'univers des déchirures et des dentelles frémissantes
Toi qui portes le son comme un nourrisson
Toi qui fais courir la lune sans arriver à faire trembler l'arc-en-ciel
Vent du large
Toi dont le souffle égal et la rumeur chantante
Bercent endorment tes adorateurs maritimes
Le jour
Toi qui renverses à minuit sur les hommes
La grande urne de l'insomnie la sueur des cauchemars et l'éboulement
écraseur
de l'angoisse
Tant tu pleures et gémis
Vent noir des nuits dans ta solitude affreuse Ecorché
Toi qui sèches les larmes
Toi qui sèches le linge
Terreur des bouts de papier des concierges des navigateurs timorés des
insectes des caravaniers des armateurs des armatures de parapluie des
ornements de la toilette féminine de certaines grosses bêtes et des personnes
sensibles et nerveuses
Toi qui réjouis les pilleurs d'épaves et le pétrel des tempêtes les cheveux
lyriques les gouttes d'eau et les poussières qui dansent le pollen amoureux le
frisson des moissons le cerfvolant le camp-volant le vol-au-vent
Et les gens peu recommandables
Je n'ai pas peur de toi
Je te dis Vent bonjour
Je te dis Bonjour Vent
Emporte mon bonjour
Au pays du Levant
Et maintenant
Vent rageant cinglant
Fous le camp
En agitant tes grands bras mous méchants
Et en courant sur tes grandes jambes pâles munies de pieds invisibles mais
gigantesques
Adieu vent
J'oubliais rendez-vous au zénith à l'auberge de la rose des vents
Et sans rancune

You wring vision out of shape
You make shivery runs and ladders in the fabric of the universe
You carry a tune like a newborn babe
You stampede the moon but can't shake the rainbow
Trade wind
You steady breather whose
daily
singsong chanty
Hypnotizes maritime devotees
Over whom at midnight you upturn
Vast urns of insomnia cold sweats nightmares and a
tidal wave of angst
Black night wind you moan and blubber as if skinned alive in your dreadful
solitude
A drier of tears
You dry wash on the line
You terrorize bits of paper
        concierges timorous navigators bugs teamsters shipwrights
            umbrella-ribs adornments of feminine toilette large animals
                and edgy thin-skinned types
You cheer the hearts of wreckers and storm petrels you jeer all else
From lyrical heads of hair dewdrops and the dance of erotic flower dust
To the shudder of harvest and the way boxkites flying columns vol au vents
and
the most unprepossessing people have of jiggling
I really am not scared of you
I say oh it's you the wind, hi there
I say Hi Wind
Say hello
To the gates of day
Now wind
You mad slasher
Get the fuck out of here
Flailing your soft puffy arms
Galloping away on those big pale gams and invisible hamlike feet
Get lost wind
Our date at the rose of the winds motel at the top of the sky
I forgot not out of spite

Mais
Si jamais
Contre l'os interdit de mon front
Tu déchaînes ta rage à la voix de tonnerre
Ta colère aux gestes d'orage
Ta vengeance ouragan
Alors ô père vent
Jusqu'à tarir ton divin sang
Plus ancien que les eaux de l'abîme océan
Jusqu'à tarir ton souffle aïeul des dieux vivants
Et fossoyeur de leurs cadavres
Jusqu'à l'effacement
De l'antique regard absent
Qui fit naître la nuit au fond de tes yeux caves
Jusqu'au silence jusqu'au blanc
Je te fouetterai vent esclave

Je te fouetterai vent

But if you ever
Go for the one bone taboo to you my forehead
Turning the air blue with your thunder
Lashing out the way you do when mad
Getting even with a cyclone
At that point papa wind
Your blood immortal and older than the abyss
I will evaporate
Your breath sole begetter of the living gods
And digger of their graves
I will exhaust
And that archaic absent gaze that makes for the
Night behind your deep-set eyes
I will extinguish
And the whiteness the stillness at the bottom of your heart
I'm going to whip out of you you slave

I'll skin you wind

Le feu du vent

Il est dit qu'avant
Les temps et les lieux

Seul le vent vivant
Tournait dans le vide

Le souffle du creux
Antérieur au coeur

Et du frottement
De son tourbillon

Naquit le point d'or
Du feu primitif

Wind Fire

They say when there was no
Such thing as time or place

The wind lived by itself
Whirling in empty space

To fill a hungry heart
Unborn with sighs until

From rubbing wind on wind
Out of the twirling gyre

There shot a golden dot
A point of flame a fire

Quand viendra le jour
du grand vent

Le vent remue à peine à la pointe du ciel
Et grandissant en soi
Se pensant plus vivant
Et plus vaste et mouvant de l'instant en l'instant
Le vent effraye
La pointe de feu du ciel Peur

Ton coeur de marbre noir ô rose d'ombre ô nuit
Nourrit par sursauts étouffants trop brusqués
L'arbre tonnant de tes veines
Le spectre de corail de tes artères

Ton coeur sentant qu'on frôle en lui
Au centre cachée
La perle inconnue

Et voici le grand vent qui mêle les étages
De l'espace
Cap d'ombre au seuil des nuits d'où sortir météore
Va-et-vient d'arc-en-ciel sur le cristal du soir
Ce qui va ce qui vient c'est la hache des ailes
Décapitant l'espace ivre de lambeaux noirs
Chaos engloutissant les faces et les masques

C'est le moment du silence qui hurle Éclair
Un frisson de la terre engloutit les marées
Sous le vent des fantômes
La terre est parcourue du frisson de la mort

Aux plages hautes de l'étendue
Dans les antres d'éther du feu
Au roc bouillant céleste
Le grand vent des métamorphoses
Travaille les formes
Monstres multicolores hydres d'arc-en-ciel

Comes the Hurricane

At the top of the sky the wind barely stirring
Puffs itself up
To where it thinks it's more alive
More vast and mobile from one second to the next
And the wind terrifies
The dot of fire in the sky Fear

Your black marble heart (O shadow rose O night)
Squirts apopleptic nourishment
Up the thundrous tree of your veins
The ghost coral of your arteries

Your heart feels something reach into its
Hidden core to stroke the
Unknown pearl

And here comes the hurricane jumbling layers
Of space
Cape of shadow at the threshold of a night it shoots out of like a meteor
While a rainbow comes and goes over the crystal slab of evening
What comes and goes is a double ax on wings
Decapitating space drunk on black shreds
In a chaos engulfing every face and mask

At the moment of silence that shrieks Lightning
A tremor engulfs tides
Under a wind of phantoms
Earth shudders she's going to die

On the lofty beaches of space
In the caverns of etheric fire
On the boiling rock of heaven
The hurricane change
Carves shapes
Gaudy monsters rainbow hydras
Stars of sea and sky

Monstres multicolores hydres d'arc-en-ciel
Étoiles de mer et de ciel
Étoiles d'air séparées de l'air par nulle membrane
Changeantes et multiformes idées

Quand le grand vent pénétrera
Nul ne sait la couleur que prendra la lumière
Sur l'aspect de prodige des beaux monstres créés
Quelle éclipse de peur quels incendies d'effroi
Le grand vent allumera
Aux espaces inférieurs où rôde le soleil
Roi des bas-mondes.

Stars of air no skin divides from air
Figments polymorphous and fickle

When the hurricane gets inside
Nobody knows what color light is going to take to illuminate
The prodigious appearance of the lovely monsters it creates
What a ghastly eclipse what a conflagration of terror
The hurricane will light
In the lower depths where the sun
King of the nether regions prowls

Le vent d'après
le vent d'avant

Depuis jamais
Je sais toujours
Souvenir d'avenir après toute vie révolue
Prévision d'autrefois d'avant tout mouvement
Avant que soit
Le premier mouvement le vent
Pour quel crime immense inconnu
D'un juge qui n'est que moi-même
Ma condamnation au présent à perpétuité
Éternité
Depuis jamais
Je sais toujours
Prévoir me souvenir du vent qui vient de plus loin que la lune
Et les étoiles
Le vent de bêtes légion
Qui glisse de plus loin que l'humaine illusion de tout l'espace oblong
Le vent de bêtes et de griffes
Qui hurlent dans les caves du ciel
Déchirent des lambeaux de soie noire aux parois supérieures de l'éther
Le vent qui vient de plus loin que tout l'espace plein
Le granit d'un seul grain de granit
Granit sans grains
Le granit plein
Le vent qui vient de plus loin que l'éternelle limite
Où le marbre est perméable au tulle
Et les étoiles alvéoles perméables à l'éther dentelles
Le vent qui n'a jamais dépassé
L'ourlet croquant de mon oreille
Le vent qui n a jamais pénétré sous mon crâne
Jamais fait résonner les grottes de mes tempes
Le vent qui secoue l'étendue onduleuse de tout
Mais le vent qui ne peut secouer moi le vide
Le trou d'absence dans le monde

Wind After
Wind Before

Forever now
I've had
Memories of a future after each past life
Premonitions of a time earlier than motion
And of the first thing that ever moved
Wind
So for what unknown atrocity
Did my judge who was none other than I myself
Pass a sentence of life in the here and now
Eternity on me
Forever now
Always I've had
Second sight memory of a
Wind out of a deeper space than moon and stars
The legion animal wind
Skittering in from beyond man's oblong illusion of the whole of space
A wind of clawing animals
Roaring in the cellars of heaven
Clawing black silk in the tall reaches of the ether
Wind out of a space deeper than the whole universe en bloc
Granite a single stony molecule
Granite submolecular
Granite solid
Wind out of a space steeper than the edge of eternity
Where marble seeps through mesh
And stars honeycomb the lacy ether
Wind that never made it past
The crackling vestibule of my ear
Wind that never got inside my head
Or made the hollows of my temples ring
Buffeting the wavy surface of it all
Wind though that can't the vacuum me
My absence a hole punched in the universe

Le défaut du cristal le crachat de l'émeraude
L'entonnoir le trou

Espace que détient mon corps statufié dans l'espace
Mon corps est le seul lieu où je ne me sais pas
Le seul lieu où je ne sois pas
Moi qui suis le vent d'avant tout mouvement
Le vent vivant après toute vie révolue
Le vent qui vient de plus loin que la forme oculaire de l'infini de l'homme
Limite de souffrance la peau la seule opacité
Nuit du tambour increvable
Que les volcans du vent fassent éclater mon crâne
Retournez-moi comme un gant
Dévaginez-moi jetez-moi nu tout vif écorché
à l'amour souterrain de l'ombre de l'envers du monde

Arrachez la viande de mes joues
Pour que je voie enfin mon rire de mort

A flaw in crystal a crackle in emerald
A funnel a hole a

Space prisoning my body carved in space
Body being the one place I have no sense of being
The only place I don't exist
I who am wind from before all motion
Wind alive after the last life passes away
Wind out of a deeper space than any human wonder-eye infinity
Limit of pain skin the one thing nobody sees through
Night of the unbreakable drum
Let volcanoes of wind blow my head open
Like a glove inside out
Gut me throw me skinned alive and as I am
        to the mines of love in the shadow
            of the earth's dark side

Rip the flesh off my face
So I can see at last how a dead man grins

L'incantation perpétuelle

Ce masque atroce instantané
La stupeur-solitude
Le fige à la surface
Du vieux torrent de chairs en chairs
accidentelles

Ce masque atroce instantané
De stupeur-solitude
Ta face

Que la grande rafale l'efface en fasse
Un néant brillant un vide éclatant
aveugle-voyant des ténèbres blanches
Etre à jamais la proie du vent

The Perpetual Incantation

That awful mask a snapshot
Amazed solitude
Transfixes on the surface
Of a perennial torrent flesh
casual flesh

The awful mask a mugshot
Of drugged solitude
Your face

May the rainburst erase it replace it
With a vacuity that shines
A dazzle of nonentity a
sightless clairvoyant of white shadows
One forever eaten by wind

Le pôle Sud

SONNET

Clamant comme un corbeau dans le silence austral
Le vent du Sud hurlait sur la vaste Antartide
Et jetait un linceul sur les steppes arides
D'obscurité lugubre en un ciel sépulcral

Tel un spectre sanglant jetant son cri fatal
Il passait, secouant de son aile morbide
L'eau glauque qui se plaint et la glace livide
Aboyant dans la nuit le cri du noir chacal

Dans les déchirements des nuages funèbres
Brillait la Croix du Sud comme l'oeil des ténèbres
Sur la froide pâleur des immenses glaçons

Qui montent à l'assaut des rochers solitaires
Échine monstrueuse où courent des frissons
Sinistres craquements troublant la Nuit Polaire!

The South Pole

SONNET

Cawing like a crow in the austral hush
The South wind shrieked across Antarctica
On whose wasteland casting a pall of such
Lugubrious gloom only a sepulchre

Could be darker it blew with fatal cries
From piercing screeches to bloodthirsty cackles
On sad-eyed melt pools and pillars of ice
As livid as a million screaming jackals

Funereal clouds parted in the sky
And the Southern Cross glittered like the eye
Of chaos at the immense pale assault

Of glaciers on the shivering stony height
That monstrous spine tuned to a shrill-pitched fault
Whose threatening music troubles Polar Night!

La tempête des cygnes
ou
La conquête des signes

Lorsque les bleus Enfants trop naïfs vont se pendre
Aux chimériques bras d'une idole imbécile
Aux cornes d'un trois-mâts maléfique & fossile
Pour abriter leur coeur de soleil dans la cendre

Souvent, ayant caressé les fleurs autochtones
Trop longtemps au départ, ils vieillissent avant
D'avoir brûlé leurs doigts au moindre galhauban,
Et vont se momifier au sel noir de l'Automne

Car ils n'ont pas connu les dangers que prépare
Aux coeurs trop purs le culte illusoire du blanc
Le blanc pourrit dans l'oeuf lorsqu'il est ovipare
Pourrissent les couleurs comme pourrit le blanc

Le soleil qui se lève a besoin de béquilles,
L'horizon se contourne aux chants d'un scrofuleux,
Les rois boivent sans soif des alcools sulfureux
Mais nous avons caché le tonnerre en nos quilles.

Noirs comme des culs
Dahoméens appartenant aux sarcophages
Où dorment les Obis de plumes revêtus
             Blancs comme la rage
Et les fruits pourrissant dans leurs mains d'or velu
Ont l'odeur du destin que nous avons voulu.

The Tempest of Swans
or
The Conquest of Signs*

When the blue Children of Innocence lashed
Themselves to the mast of a jinxed square-rigger
Or to the pedestal of some cult figure
To hide the day-star of their heart in ash

The flowers in their back yard they mooned over
Too long, and never did sail, never burned
Beneath a tropic sun but only aged, turned
To mummies in the black salt of October

Oblivious to the dangers that viviparous
Lilywhite hearts incur because of race
The white runs in the ovum when oviparous
And addles at the sight of a black face.

This morning's sun can only rise on crutches,
The horizon wobbles, making some folks ill;
The kings are sipping hot gin in their hutches,
But you and I stow thunder in our fo'c'stle,

Black as assholes
Of Dahomeyan hoodoo-men at tombs
Where obeahs sleep in cerements of plumes.
White as castles
Of rage where hands covered with golden down
heft fruit near-rotten
Smelling of the fate we have always
hoped for and now gotten.

*Lines in italics by René Daumal

Or un éléphant nain ...

Or un éléphant nain souriait dans la lune
Pauvre petit à peine issu du lupanar
Tout englué, tout parfumé de spika-nard,
Enténébré de l'heure où va courir la rune.

Fils d'un lémure simple d'esprit, d'une amibe
Aussi d'eau douce que dodue, et du Chacal
Mangeur de morts au fumet ammoniacal
Qui pourrissait au flanc noir de sa diatribe.

Ce n'est pas tout car un toutou lui tient de père
— le Toutou vert de l'eau putride où va le vent
Plangorer comme l'oeuf d'un vieil engoulevent—
Et voici venir, à petits pas, sa grand-mère.

Oh! la douce sardine à l'oeil plein de lumière!
Oh! généalogie où court mon désespoir!
Quand je songe qu'un archangel était son hoir
J'ai peur de ne tisser jamais plus la lisière!

Son plus beau pyjama (camisole de force
En peau de bouc, et teinte de bleu céladon)
—Mort aux rats, mes amis, et vive l'amidon!—
Il l'avait étendu sur son doux petit torse.

Son petit torse torse et tortillé, doux être!
Doux être glapissant tel le Crapaud de mes
Rêves d'enfant chéri des Alcyons charmés—
Vois surgir le Dément qui t'emmènera paître!

Hélas! Hélas! Il est celui des soirs d'angoisse
Celui des soirs de glace, où l'iceberg en deuil
Sanglote ses stalactites fines au seuil
Du rêve pantelant où tout se plaque et poisse.

Midget Elephant*

A midget elephant smirked at the moon
Just out the cathouse door and still quite sticky
Reeking of spikenard, tweaking his doohickey
He struck the hour of the mystic rune.

An imbecilic lemur, an amoeba
Kind and fat, a carrion-eating jackal
Emitting scents faintly ammoniacal
From digging in a graveyard like a beaver.

These were the family, along with Pater
Whose farts smelt like an addled nightjar egg
Cracked over a moldy butter keg—
He tiptoed in with Granny somewhat later.

What a sweet sardine to a light-filled eye!
What a family! Imagine my despair
Recalling an archangel was his heir—
A tapestry I'll never weave, said I.

His best pajamas—they were a buckskin
Straitjacket dyed institutional green
(Death to rats, gentlemen, and long live starch!)
He pulled gingerly on over his parts.

Chico I see you as you are at last you're
Quite like the barking Toad I dreamt of once
The scion of enchanted Halcyons—
A lunatic will put you out to pasture.

And as your good intentions go kerflooey
A grieving iceberg silently appears
Shedding the fine stalactites of her tears
In dreams where you wake up all soft and gooey.

*Lines in italics by René Daumal

O sang coagulé de la lune frigide
S'éternisant en glas dans les limbes d'orfroi
Le ciel est plat et gras, qui distille l'effroi
Noir et chaud dans mon crâne horrible qui se vide

Sur la nuit d'externat l'éléphant se décalque
Et l'escargot, jouant du saxophone, tel
Pyrrhus au bord du Gange, —ennui sacramentel!—
Oh! l'ennui bleu qui tombe autour du catafalque.

Hors du jupon froissé, dressant sa trompe nue
Il bondit. Alors se passa la Chose. Soit! —
Taisons-nous, Sabaoth! si l'éléphant déçoit
L'attente du cosmos, immanez sa venue!

Lecomte - Daumale
Classe d'Histoire
Décembre 24

70

The moon congealing to a bloody clot
Goes ding-a-ling (hell's bells in a gilt-edged limbo)
Where pop go the brain cells alas poor bimbo
She spills the beans and they are black and hot.

Lest Jumbo reawakening appear
A Pyrrhic snail playing the saxophone
On the banks of the Ganges rolls his own;
Blue Ennui collapses at the bier.

His naked trunk lifting a rumpled slip
The elephant charges, last but not least—
Silence, O Sabaoth, before the beast
Frustrates a yearning cosmos, let 'er rip!

Lecomte-Daumale
History Class
December '24

Le taureau noir

Je suis un fantoche en baudruche
Avec un visage de craie
Et des yeux de brique pilée.
Je descends dans l'ombre, en flottant,
L'étroitesse d'un escalier,
Puis, sur le point mort d'un palier,
Vacille d'épouvantement.
Le diable, gnou sans queue et apte
A claudiquer sur ses deux pattes
Sardoniquement me regarde
Avec de longs yeux qui ricanent.
Son col cambré se détandant
Propulse soudain contre moi
Son chef trop fin de taureau noir,
Totem hiératique en carton

Il fuit, enlaçant à ses cornes
Mes tripailles en banderoles.

The Black Bull

I'm a puppet of goldbeater's skin
With my chalky face
And brick powder eyes
Mincing down a staircase
In the dark
To a landing where
Startled I lurch back as
Satan a tailless wildebeest
Comes clumping up the stairs, his
Sardonic slit-eyes smiling into mine.
Stretching an arched neck
He springs forward
In his effetely fine-featured
Bull mask of black cardboard

Then retreats, having entwined my guts
In streamers on his horns

Les quatre éléments

à Rolland de Renéville.

Si je dis Feu mon corps est entouré de flammes
Je dis Eau l'Océan vient mourir à mes pieds

Vaisseau vide immergé dans un cristal solide
Creuse momie aux glaces prises et je dis Air

Terre et le naufragé prend racine et s'endort
Sous les feuilles au vent de l'arbre de son corps

De sa bouche le songe engendre un rameau d'or
De sa bouche terreuse expirant ses poumons
Retournés vers le ciel tonnante frondaison

Moisson rouge au soleil de minuit et de mort

The Four Elements

to Rolland de Renéville

If I say Fire I am ringed in flames
When I say Water Ocean expires at

My feet an empty hull floating in solid
Crystal a mummy on ice is Air

In Earth the castaway takes root sleeping
Under the leafy tree of his own body

The dream's golden branch shoots out his mouth
A dirt-caked mouth exhaling to the sky
From lungs inside out like booming treetops

Red harvest in the mortal midnight sun

Tétanos mystique

I

(NUIT VIVANTE D'ALEXANDRIE)

Irréelle dans sa blancheur d'âme tarie
Par de trop lourds parfums—sel d'une mer lustrale—
Voici la maladive nuit, la nuit trop pâle.

Voici la nuit où luit jadis Alexandrie!
L'esprit divague, usé par tant de fleurs bizarres,
Par tant d'étrangetés, d'excès de savoirs rares.

C'est l'astrale splendeur de nuit sur l'eau marine
Où clairement se mire une lune falotte.

A l'horizon d'opale une étoile sanglote,
Trou dans le ciel, d'où l'infini vers l'eau s'incline.

II

(PANTHÉISME)

Las! depuis des temps et des temps
Dont s'exaspère la longueur
Et la nostalgie en mon coeur,
Sans un autre désir, j'attends.

J'attends les immortels instants,
Où, délivré de ma rancoeur,
Je serai, centre du grand choeur,
La Monade vers qui je tends . . .

Il est dit que le pèlerin
Des chemins de nuit et d'airain,
A l'heure où son âme comprend

Mystic Tetanus

I

(THE LIVING NIGHT OF ALEXANDRIA)

Her soul is dry and impossibly white,
Bleached in the perfumes of a lustral sea—
You're looking at a sickness when you see

The lights of Alexandria by night
Having studied so many arcane plants,
Secrets, rarities, you are in a trance;

And the moon's even paler than you thought her,
For at the opaline horizon's vent

A tearful star punctures the firmament,
Infinity heels over in deep water.

II

(PANTHEISM)

Alas, nostalgia overpowers
Me and how easily I tire.
Dead to any other desire
I live only for the rare hours.

The immortal moments when I do
Transcend all bitterness, all fear,
And reach the center of the sphere,
The Monad I aspire to

On those paths of which it is written
In the dark wind if not in brass,
That at the bottom of a smitten

Les métempsycoses que lui
Impose l'infini, se rend
Au point d'où l'Unité a lui!

III

(NICOLAÏSME)

Va, Banni! —le corps s'hallucine
Aux nuits des sens. Surtout, médite
Sur tout le néant qu'on habite,
—Seule vaut l'âme cristalline.

Mais pour tuer les sens j'incline
Vers une foi nicolaïte
Hérétique et sept fois maudite.
(On se damne quand on raffine!)

Au lieu d'ascétisme stérile
Je crois que le corps s'annihile
Aussi bien aux poisons des vices,

Mon âme je me réfugie,
Pour te délivrer des supplices,
Dans la plus homicide orgie!

IV

(MANICHÉISME)

Monstrueux prophète Manès,
Pour aimer ses rites et ses
Conscientes malignités,
Hélas!: Manê, Thecel, Phares,

Je me meurs de ton népanthès
Ah, croire en tes dualités!

Heart the traveler comes to grasp
A link unbroken with the night,
Eternity burst into light.

III

(NICOLAITANISM)

Think, outcast, how the flesh can crawl
In the night of the senses, though
Nothing is real except to flow
In the crystal stream of the soul.

To quell the senses I incline
Still, like old Nicholas, to hold
With heresies damned sevenfold:
To burn in Hell is to refine.

So let not sterile abstinence
But the lye of incontinence
Take all—that you, my soul, my higher

Self may escape the lake of fire
I want to flame out in a flood
Of crime, a cloud of sperm and blood.

IV

(MANICHEISM)

That Mani was a monstrous person
Much as I adore his rite, he
epitomized malignity—
Mene mene tekel upharsin—

I drank his famed nepenthe all for
Naught. Spare me his duality,

Quel ragoût de perversité,
Au goût de soufre et d'aloès.

Je me voue à Satan. Pourtant
Satan qui va toujours luttant,
Quand seront consommés les temps,

Croulera, vaincu, par le fer.
Qu'importe, morbide, j'attends
D'aller ululer en enfer!

V

(NUIT MORTE D'ALEXANDRIE)

Ame d'Alexandrie,—Oh, ton âme nocturne
Subtile et raffinée et lasse et taciturne,
—Tu n'es plus maintenant, sur un désert, que vide.

L'eau reflète une absence, à jamais dans sa moire,
La folie, en chaos, souffle, basphématoire,
Où ton art paroxysme a vibré : mort livide,

Qui gît, hallucinant, dans la ténèbre verte.
Où chantaient les parfums, râle un goût de poussière;

Et l'astre vacillant dont blémit la lumière,

That ragout of perversity
Compounded of aloes and sulfur.

I prefer Satan. He may well
Bite the dust in the end, it's true;
He won't go down without a fight,

Though, and we'll take some with us, too,—
I can't wait for the sheer delight
Of howling next to him in Hell.

V

(THE DEAD NIGHT OF ALEXANDRIA)

Though Alexandria could be in turn
Dark, deep, weary, witty, or taciturn
The desert shows no traces of her soul.

The sea reflects its absence, chaos rages
Against the light and there are no more sages,
Only a madman babbling in a hole;

For she is dead,—in the green shady place
Where her perfumes sang, mute dust fills the mouth

And you can see in that star fading out
A doorway opening in empty space.

Au vent du Nord

Tu vis, tu ne vis pas tu rampes dans la pierre
Prisonnier d'un songe
Amant dans un rêve
Écrasé d'avance
Par le trop lourd corps-mort
De marbre de ta mort
Que tu cherches hurlant depuis des millénaires
Dans les ravages et les cadavres de ton corps
Alerte épouvantail claire-voie au vent du nord
Dansant et suant de vertige
Sur un sol d'air fuyard où ton poids c'est la peur

Coeur éclaté vidé de sang et de sanglots
Pris au gel de l'air
Sous le ciel de pierre
A jamais emmuré dans un cristal de froid

To the North Wind

Alive yet not alive you crawl in stone
Prisoner of an air castle
Lover in a dream
Crushed in advance
By the heavy heavy
Marble anchor of the
Death you have been howling for for a hundred centuries
In the ravages and corpses you embody
Alert scarecrow wicket in the north wind
Giddily dancing in a cold sweat
On a footing of slippery air where your weight is the weight of fear

A burst heart empty of blood and woe
Caught in frozen air
At the stony edge of space
Sealed for eternity in the crystal icebox of the sky.

L'éternité en un clin d'oeil

à Arthur Adamov

Quiconque voit son double en face doit mourir

Échéance du drame au voyant solitaire
Miroir un oeil regarde un oeil qui le regarde
Offert et renoncé pur don et dur refus
D'étrangère qui n'en peut plus qui n'en peut plus
Donatrice abreuvée aux sources des insultes

Hantise du reflet glacial ombre vaine
De ce double avéré plus soi-même que soi
Simulacre nié de menteuse lumière
Perdue aux ondes d'ombre aux sombres eaux de mort

Miracle du regard regardant l'oeil qui darde
Un inverse regard vigilant assassin
Provocateur
Assassinat se dit suicide au jeu mortel

Immortelle qui passe à travers le miroir
Pupille que contracte un acte pur détruire
C'est l'étoile-fantôme à l'âme de feu noir
Le point nul en son propre intérieur vibrant

L'oeil dévorera l'oeil au point nul éternel

Eternity in a Wink

to Arthur Adamov

Whoever sees their double face to face

Has got to die it's curtains for the hermit seer
An eye looking at an eye that looks back in the mirror
An offer drop it clean offer mean rebuff
By an alien who "had enough" she said
Provider slaked with insults at the source

It's an obsession a cold shadow the
Empty reflection of this self-styled double who is more "you" than you are
Fraud disowned of perjured light
Abstracted in the black welter of a lethal elixir

It's a miracle that an eye shooting a look of hatred
Can be held in a reciprocally
Vigilant and murderous gaze the stare of a provocateur
Suicide means murder in this game

To pass immortal through the looking glass
Pupils contract it's a clean act destruction
Each stab a ghost star with a soul of black fire
A zero point in its own pulsing core

At the last zero point eternity eye eats eye

L'oeuf mystique

... Et quand fut consommé le cycle des souffrances
Réfugié au Sud-extrême, il attendit
Parmi la beauté nue et froide de la nuit
Corps astral immense et léger prêt aux absences.

Fluide étrangement, presque immatériel
Il sentait le roulis berceur de la planète
Qui roule, errante épave en le gouffre du ciel.
Puis ce fut le départ à l'essor de comète.

Il grandit, absorba dans une apothéose
Les étoiles sans fin, jusqu'à devenir tout,
Jusqu'à devenir l'être infini. Tout à coup,
Il entrevit au loin, réalité morose,

Ce qui rêve à travers le principe éternel,
D'où le verbe émana qui parla la matière,
Violet dans le noir absolu, étant tel
                Un Oeuf énorme de Lumière!

The Mystic Egg

... And when the cycle of his sufferings ended
From an Antarctic refuge he ascended
Into the cold nude beauty of the night
Expanding, full of holes, immense yet light

So light that he was almost immaterial
Though strangely fluid—he could feel the soft
Rolling of earth that ghost ship in the ethereal
Abyss—then cometlike he shot aloft

And grew still more until swallowing up
Whole galaxies and universes he
Usurped the being of infinity,—
At that moment reality went pop

And in the distance suddenly he saw
The one whose dreaming is eternal law
Whose utterance fecund in the dark of night
                    Is a giant Egg of violet light!

Dans les yeux de la nuit

Une femme s'endort sur un toit c'est la nuit
Abandonnée antique au péril du vertige
Aux traîtrises rêveuses des gestes du sommeil
Songeuse ensevelie en glissades mortelles
Sur le haut toit déserte glace tendue face à l'espace
Sur le zinc oxydé de vieux soleil tueur
Et de lune ancienne empoisonneuse en larmes
La grande somnambule y crie de tous ses ongles
De ses doigts déments naissent des diamants crissants
Et des gouttes de sang qui chantent en dansant
La danse en perles du mercure
Vers la femme qui dort sur le monstre du vide
Une cheminée fume un nuage en haillons
Dans la soie noire de la suie le vent des nuits
Dresse une tente errante
Creuse l'antre céleste nomade
Pour l'adoration des yeux prodigieux
De la femme endormie aux paupières battantes
Ses trop longs cils vibrants émeuvent les rayons
Des étoiles rétractiles
C'est la nuit la dormeuse un oeil clos l'autre ouvert
Tout le monde à jouer contre ce qu'elle voit.

Into the Eyes of Night

A woman dozes on a roof her name is night
Ancient abandoned to the perils of intoxication
To sleep's fumbling treasons
Dreamer in an avalanche of slips
Ditched on a high glassy place to eyeball outer space
Over the corroded zinc where old man sun the killer
And his old lady that tearful poisoner the moon tend bar
Our big sleepwalker's nails screech all at once
Her fingers sprout insanely squealing diamonds
Drops of blood singing in midair
Dance like beads of mercury
Up to this woman curled in the monster's lap of nothingness
A chimney fumes a cloud in tatters
In sooty black silk the night wind
Pitches a nomad tent
Lining heaven a celestial floater
In the sleeper's huge adoring
Eyes their lids stirring as
Long long lashes flutter and
Shrinking stars explode
The name is night she sleeps with one eye open
And all the world at stake on what she sees

La sainte enfance:
ou
Suppression de la naissance

Je parlerai du noir
Poupée de porcelaine
Enfouie dans l'humus de la forêt oublieuse et traîtresse
Où dansent les squelettes en robes d'araignées
Des feuilles mortes en dentelles
Je parlerai du noir
Au souffle des cavernes
Dans la champignonnière aux yeux phosphorescents
Je parlerai du noir aux escargots noués
Je parlerai du noir
A la pluie à la suie
Au cercle d'eau de lune étalé au fond du puits
Aux tonneaux qui roulaient dans la cave à minuit
Quand la dame blanche gémit
Je parlerai du noir
A l'envers des miroirs
Je parlerai du noir
De l'immortel tourment
Du plus vieux désespoir
Devant le monde absent
Alors qu'il fera blanc
Je parlerai de voir
Toujours en m'endormant
Cette femme endormie
Sur la terre en pleurant
Admirable tête de morte
Voilée de noir espoir d'enfance assassinée
Un mauvais regard bat des ailes
Près du lit vide ensanglanté
Il faudra pendre l'accouchée
Pour le crime ancien des limbes
Le mort-né retourné vers son lieu d'origine
Ne croira pas au jour menti par le soleil
    L'air noir n'a pas souillé le seuil de sa poitrine

Holy Childhood
or
Concealment of Birth

I'll speak of the dark:
China doll
Buried in the floor of a false forgetful forest
Where skeletons dressed as spiders dance
Lacework of dead leaves
I'll speak of the dark
To dank caves
Mushroom beds eyes glowing in the blackness
I'll speak of the dark to coiled snails
I'll speak of the dark
To rain to soot
To the circle of moonwater motionless at the bottom of a well
To barrels rolling in the cellar at midnight
When the white lady moaned
I'll speak of the dark
On the blind side of mirrors
I'll speak of the dark
Of immortal torture
Of most ancient despair
In the absence of a universe
And should a light shine
I'll speak of the light
I always see when falling asleep
That woman stretched
On the ground weeping
An admirable death's head
Veiled in black the murdered hope of childhood
An evil scowl flaps its wings
Next to the empty blood-soaked bed
The mother will have to hang
For the crime of a former life
Restored to its point of origin the stillborn child
Will never believe the lie of broad daylight
    Black air never entered its lungs

91

Sans que palpite sa narine
Sans que son oeil s'entr'ouvre à l'atroce réveil
La vie reniée avant d'être
Il s'en retourne au lieu de naître
Par le fil qui relie le nombril au zénith
Aux sources de cristal des merveilles du vide

Without making its nostrils quiver and its eyes
Widen at the horror of awakening
Having let go of life before even existing
It returns to the place it came from
By a thread linking its belly button to the top of the sky
To crystal fountains of wondrous emptiness

Je veux être confondu ...
ou
La halte du prophète

à Claude Sernet

Vous vous trompez je ne suis pas celui qui monte
Je suis l'autre toujours celui qu'on n'attend pas
Ma face sous le masque rouge gloire et honte
Tourne au vent que je veux pour seul guide à mes pas
J'assumerai l'immobilité des statues
Sous la colère de l'orage anx gestes tors
Qui rompt au sol vos fronts ruines abattues
Mais me laisse debout n'ayant raison ni tort
Qu'espérez-vous de moi seul droit dans la tourmente
Terriblement absent roide et froid sans sommeil
Pour parler aux vieux morts il faut trouver la fente
Par où filtre un rayon noir de l'autre soleil
Et si je tombe avant le soir sur la grand'route
La face contre terre et les deux bras en croix
Du fond de tout l'influx de force sourd en moi
Je me redresserai pour la nuit des déroutes
Et je remonterai vers vous comme la voix
Des grandes eaux hurlant sous les nocturnes voûtes
Avant l'heure et le signe advenus laissez-moi
Laissez-moi seul vous tous qui niez le prophète
Transmuant toute vie en un retournement
Du sens illuminé par d'immortels tourments
Laissez-moi dans le vide atroce de ma tête
Confondant confondu confondu confondant

I Want to be Damned
or
Where the Prophet Stopped

to Claude Sernet

You're wrong I'm not the one that went up I'm
Still the other guy the man no man looks for
My face behind the red mask glory shame
Faces the wind wind is my only guide
I'll stand there like a statue even as
Some crazy gust knocks down a ruined house
Leaving me upright forget about right
What do you want of me the only one
Standing yet cold numb restless not all there
To reach persons long dead go for the crack
Black light from the other sun filters through
And if ere evening I happen to fall
Flat on my face in the road arms outstretched
A jolt of the old juice my ultimate
Will bring me to my feet for the defeat
Night will hasten as I howl in a voice like
Great waters growling in the vault of night
Until the coming of that sign that hour
Leave me alone go on deny a prophet's
Power to turn life inside out transmuting
All sense to an immortal flash of pain
Leave me to the horrors inside my empty
Head and they are damning damned damned damning

Testament

Je viens de loin de beaucoup plus loin
    Qu'on ne pourrait croire
Et les confins de nuit des déserts de la faim
    Savent seuls mon histoire
Avec ses ongles avec ses dents celle qui est partout
    M'a fait mal
Et surtout surtout son affreux regard de boue
    M'a fait mal
Si maintenant je dors ancré
    Au port de la misère
C'est que je n'ai jamais su dire assez
    A la misère
Je suis tombé en bas du monde
    Et sans flambeau
Sombré à fond d'oubli plein de pitiés immondes
    Pour moi seul beau

Testament

I come from afar in the marches of night
 Much farther than one might imagine
My story is slight in the city of light
 Well known in the deserts of famine
With her teeth and her nails she's everywhere
 I let her mangle me
But her eyes say I'm a piece of slime
 And she will strangle me
And if my berth tonight I choose
 In the havens of misery since
I never knew how to refuse
 Misery's blandishments
To the bottom of the heap I slide
 With neither pisspot nor candle
But oblivion's obscene solicitudes
 To me alone a lovely scandal

La tête couronnée

Délire don tonnant du songe et des écumes
Anneau d'onde vibrante au creux futur virginité
Entre moi-même et le néant qui m'a hanté
Ma tête ballottante au vent en vol de plumes
Étincelante au choc des marteaux sur l'enclume
S'éblouit de son sort d'or pur immérité
L'assaut des marteaux l'environne
Sur son front forge sa couronne
Cercle ardent sacerdoce infamant du malheur
A grands coups de douleur ruisselante écarlate
J'ai peur qu'à force de splendeur
La tête éclate

Crowned Head

Madness thundery gift of dream and dross
Ring where the cave of the future rings
Cherry between me and the boogeyman Nothingness
My wind-tossed head a flurry of feathers
Shoots sparks as hammers strike anvil
Dazzled by undeserving pure gold fortune
Stormy hammers surround it
Crown it with the fresh forged
Hot circlet of the infamous calling of misfortune
In chunks of dripping scarlet pain
I'm terrified all this splendor
Will make it pop

A Chronology of the Life of
Roger Gilbert-Lecomte

1907   Roger Lecomte born on 18 May in Reims.

1920   Enters lycée in Reims.

1921   First poems. With schoolmates starts a magazine, *Apollo;* is editor-in-chief.

1922   The 14-year-old René Daumal arrives in Reims.

1923   Lecomte, Daumal, and others form a group, Les Simplistes; experiments with carbon tetrachloride.

1924   The Simplistes experiment with out-of-body experiences (carbon tetrachloride, ether, opium); discovery of Surrealism and automatic writing.

1925   Daumal begins studying Sanskrit; Lecomte develops first morphine habit, aided by a pharmacist's daughter.

1926   Lecomte begins medical studies; meets future patron Léon Pierre-Quint; sojourn in Paris; meets Czech painter Joseph Sima, a lifelong influence and friend (Sima illustrated Lecomte's works both in his lifetime and posthumously; Lecomte wrote two major essays on Sima). By the end of this year Lecomte is addicted to opium.

1927   Experiments with extraretinal vision at René Maublanc's apartment; Lecomte attends medical school in Reims. Grand Jeu (Great Game) group is founded. The group name invented by Roger Vailland; weekly meetings chez Joseph Sima.

1928   *Grand Jeu* No. 1 (magazine) comes out in March. Lecomte travels in North Africa, gives lecture on Grand Jeu in Algiers. Changes name from Lecomte to Gilbert-Lecomte.

1929   Surrealists summon Grand Jeu group to meeting "to study possibilities of joint action" (March). *Grand Jeu* No. 2.

1930   Surrealists attempt to coopt Lecomte and Daumal; Daumal is publicly wooed by Breton; rebuffs Surrealist advances in an open letter to Breton. Lecomte is hospitalized in clinics for withdrawal from drugs several times this year. Daumal finishes *Le Contre-ciel (Coun-*

terheaven); starts relationship with Véra Milanova. *Grand Jeu* No. 3.

1931   *Grand Jeu* No. 4, its theme "experimental metaphysics," is ready for the printers but fails to come out. (It never did appear until the 1977 reprint of the whole of *Grand Jeu* magazine.) Group beginning to disintegrate. Lecomte is detoxed several times. When off drugs he drinks heavily. In September, Daumal and Véra take Lecomte in, in order to help him withdraw from his opiate addiction, a disastrous enterprise; in October he is hospitalized, gravely ill, to be confined to his bed at home in Reims, where his mother takes care of him until the following spring. In November, Daumal moves toward Gurdjieff; he tries unsuccessfully to convert fellow members of Grand Jeu group, including Lecomte.

1932   Grand Jeu group goes into final crisis; involvement in "Aragon Affair." (Louis Aragon had published a revolutionary poem which the government considered seditious; he was being prosecuted under laws targeting advocacy of violent overthrow of the state; Lecomte signed the petition to dismiss charges.) In late spring, Lecomte recovers from his long illness and by August has written most of the poems in *Life Love Death Void and Wind*. Fall: formal dissolution of Grand Jeu. December: Daumal leaves for New York City as press agent for Uday Shankar, the Hindu dancer. Lecomte delivers a lecture at the Sorbonne, with Artaud in the audience: "The Metamorphoses of Poetry." Lecomte joins the Association of Revolutionary Artists and Writers, together with Breton, Crevel, et al.

1933   January: Death of Lecomte's mother. Lecomte arrested with a drug dealer; hospitalized. On leaving hospital he spends inheritance on drugs and an addict girlfriend. He meets Ruth Kronenberg. Daumal returns from New York. October: Publication of *Life Love Death Void and Wind*.

1934   Daumal breaks off his friendship with Lecomte: "The relationship was broken off by me when I at last saw that its hidden objective and visible results were to mutually justify us in our respective weaknesses, to exempt each of his responsibilites in the other's eyes, and to make it easier for both of us to avoid looking at reality. A number of circumstances and real friendships helped me to precipitate this break, yet it was quite painful" (Letter to Paulhan, 1937). In the same letter, Daumal commends himself as one of the few Grand

Jeu members who had not abandoned the quest for truth that originally animated the group: "Most of the others have turned into party hacks, mystics, fanatics, suicides, or maniacs." December: Artaud's review of *Life Love Death Void and Wind* appears in the *Nouvelle Revue Française*.

1935   Daumal's *Counterheaven* wins the Jacques Doucet Prize. Book is dedicated to Lecomte. Lecomte living on rue Friant, on the outskirts of Paris, with Ruth Kronenberg; wants to marry her but is forbidden by father; she supports him by working as a seamstress.

1937   Daumal's *Night of Serious Drinking,* a fictionalized account of Grand Jeu times, is published. Lecomte arrested for dealing drugs; sentenced to four months imprisonment, suspended, and 300 francs fine. At around this time Lecomte may possibly have visited friends in Ireland.

1938   Lecomte's *Black Mirror* is published. Beginning of Lecomte's close friendship with Arthur Adamov, whom he has known for the past decade.

1939   Lecomte moves into a hotel on rue des Canettes, near Saint-Germain-des-Prés; arrested for dealing; his father pays fine; he moves to rue Bardinet; in December he is arrested again and imprisoned for one month.

1940   Daumal, ill with TB, marries Véra (who is Jewish) and moves with her to Marseille. Ruth Kronenberg is arrested in the *Grand Rafle* ("the big round-up") aimed at foreigners and Jews; she is released. Adamov leaves Paris, having tried unsuccessfully to persuade Lecomte to move to the Unoccupied Zone; Lecomte is found by Mme. Firmat unconscious in the street.

1941   Daumal translates Suzuki essays on Zen, a booklength collection to be published by Gallimard; guest-edits special issue of *Cahiers du Sud* on India; working on his own essays on Indian civilization and Sanskrit literature and philosophy to be published in France under the title *Bharata* (and in U.S. as *Rasa*).

1942   Ruth Kronenberg again arrested; deported to Auschwitz, never to return; Adamov comes back to Paris. Adamov and Lecomte publish a series on German Romanticism in *Comoedia* (July-November). July issue of *Nouvelle Revue Française* publishes two poems by Lecomte: "Where the Prophet Stopped" and "Vacancy in Glass" under the title "Palace of the Void." The November issue of N.R.F. publishes a review of Jouhandeau by Lecomte.

1943   Daumal returns to Paris from a two-year convalescence in the Alps for TB; working on *Mount Analogue*. 22 November: Lecomte writes to Pierre Minet, begging for assistance: "I'm rotting away, paralysed with abscesses . . . " 23 December: Lecomte is admitted as an emergency patient at Broussais hospital. 31 December at 5:45 p.m., Lecomte, unattended at Broussais hospital, dies of tetanus. His will leaves all to his father as universal legatee. Although penniless at the moment, Lecomte was on the point of being awarded a large inheritance from a recently deceased aunt.

1944   21 May: Daumal dies in Paris of TB. Special issue of *Cahiers du Sud* dedicated to Lecomte.

1955   Publication of *Testament,* a volume of selected poems by Lecomte assembled by Arthur Adamov with the permission of Lecomte, Senior. (Published by Gallimard, this volume was withdrawn from sale after the court decision authorizing publication of the Complete Works.)

1964   Association of Friends of Roger Gilbert-Lecomte's Works is founded.

1969   January: Civil Court in Reims authorizes publication of Roger Gilbert-Lecomte's *Correspondance*. Two further volumes of Prose and Poetry were to follow in 1974 and 1977.

Bibliography

The translator is indebted to Alain and Odette Virmaux's *Roger Gilbert-Lecomte et le Grand Jeu,* to date the most important biographical and critical study of Roger Gilbert-Lecomte. Grateful acknowledgment is also due Alain and Odette Virmaux for certain corrections, reconstructions, and variant versions of poems appearing in the main text of this translation.

Artaud, Antonin. Review of Roger Gilbert-Lecomte's *La Vie l'Amour la Mort le Vide et le Vent. La Nouvelle Revue Française* No. 255 (December 1934).

Dumas, Roland. *Plaidoyer pour Roger Gilbert-Lecomte.* Paris: Editions Gallimard, 1985.

Gilbert-Lecomte, Roger. *Correspondance.* Edited by Pierre Minet. Paris: Editions Gallimard, 1971.

Letters to René Daumal, Roger Vailland, René Maublanc, Véra Milanova and others.

————. *Lettre à Benjamin Fondane.* Edited by Michel Carassou. *Non Lieu,* 1985.

————. *Le Miroir Noir.* Paris: Editions Sagesse (chez Fernand Marc), 1938.

————. *Oeuvres complètes.* Proses, Volume 1. Edited by Marc Thivolet. Paris: Editions Gallimard, 1974.

————. *Oeuvres complètes.* Poésies, Volume 2. Edited by Jean Bollery. Paris: Editions Gallimard, 1977.

————. *Sacre et Massacre de l'Amour.* Paris: Editions Paul Facchetti, 1960.

Illustrated with lithographs by Joseph Sima.

————. *La Vie l'Amour la Mort le Vide et le Vent.* Paris: Editions des Cahiers Libres (Denoël, 1933.

Le Grand Jeu. Reprint (4 vols. in 1). Paris: Jean Michel Place 1977.

Numerous texts by Gilbert-Lecomte alone and in collaboration with René Daumal.

Virmaux, Alain and Odette. *Roger Gilbert-Lecomte et le Grand Jeu.* Paris: Pierre Belfond, 1981.

About the Translator

A native of East Hampton, Long Island, living in New York City, David Rattray has spent much of his life in Paris. Other published translations from French include *Difficult Death,* by René Crevel (North Point, 1986), and major portions of the *Artaud Anthology* (ed. Jack Hirschman, City Lights, 1965). His book of poems *Opening the Eyelid,* was published by *diwan* earlier this year.

Index of Titles (French)

Index of Titles (English)

Index of First Lines (French)

Index of First Lines (English)